MY MOTHER KILLED ME:

The Untold Story Of Growing Up - You Might As Well Get It All Wrong

Vanessa Miller

Table of Contents

INTRODUCTION

Growing up is difficult. Where did the time go from being woken up by Mom for school one day to driving the car for college the next? As an adult seeing a child grow up, a parent may anticipate all of the challenges that they will face. It all starts when they're learning to crawl as infants. Parents want to make sure their child is on track for success and on pace for their age group. After waking up is (literally) a walk in the park, everything else follows.

I remember what it was like growing up. My mother did everything for me, and that really affected my growth as I advance in age, and had to leave home, and be with another location. First it was college, and now leaving as an independent adult. From the lessons, and as a mother now, there are repetitions I would keep from happening, and having experienced this first hand makes me a right person to share these things, and shed light on my personal experience with some of them.

This would share necessary knowledge and awareness to mothers who wanna be the best Moms but doing everything wrong now in the name of being a lovely mother. Don't be that mother, and I want you to digest this, and have every word at the back of your minds.

To be honest, it's difficult for a parent to "back off" and let their child live their own life after teaching them so much since the day they were born.

However, independence must be attained. Having a parent handle all of a child's ups and downs leaves the child unable to deal with challenging situations.

Are they talking to their teacher about their poor grade, or is Mommy sending them threatening emails? Do they tidy their room on Saturday mornings, or does mum do it for them because they don't trust their child to do it?

When we do one thing for our child, it usually leads to five more, and although we think we're just fulfilling our motherly duties, we're actually creating a monster. And no one likes to admit to their child being spoilt – no one takes satisfaction in that statement. But they might not have to. If a parent does any of these things, they may be giving birth to the spoilt child they promised themselves they'd never have. They might be giving birth to the pampered child they promised themselves they'd never have.

WHAT YOU SHOULDN'T DO IF YOU WANT TO RAISE A GOOD CHILD - THIS IS FROM EXPERIENCE

FIGHT THEIR BATTLES FOR THEM

From time to time, little kids get into fights. It may have started with sharing in first grade, but fights can quickly escalate in middle and high school. However, getting involved is the last thing a parent should do. Fighting their fights for them is not only humiliating, but it also demonstrates that your youngster is incapable of standing up for himself.

I'll never forget being in a fight with a lover in high school, and my mother taking my phone to add her two cents... To say the least, I was horrified, and it's highly embarrassing for the other person.

BEING A BFF RATHER THAN A PARENT

The desire to be your child's best friend is alluring. It's reassuring to know that no matter what happens in life, you'll always have your "mini-me" at your side. And, while this is romanticized, it is not always reality. Your child may want to be your best friend, but they may not want to be yours. And if you're one of the small percentage of parents who are best friends with their children, you're spoiling them in an *unfixable* way. Whatever troubles your child encounters, they will not take them seriously since they know Mommy will handle the situation and make everything great.

They're additionally much less probable to get disenchanted whilst things cross awry because their fine buddy is their Mom — what could possibly go wrong?

SELECTING THEIR HAPPINESS OVER YOURS

This may disillusioned a few parents accessible, however your happiness is simply as important as your toddler's. If both you and your toddler have a free day to spend collectively, it does not need to be all approximately what they need. you are entitled to doing some thing you need to do, as nicely. whilst you're walking on low, constantly giving, giving, and giving, you have got not anything else to give at the cease of the day. you are worn-out, wiped out. Likewise, your child can even sense entitled. regardless of how their Mom is feeling, they recognize that she'll do something they need or want. After such a lot of years of giving, whilst Mom does finally say "no," who is aware of how the child's going to react.

LETTING THEM STOP LOTS OF THINGS

Whenever my mother feels like having a "proud mother" Moment, she brings up the fact that she would not let us cease matters so easily. There could be days once I wanted to end basketball, but she knew how lots I favored my teammates or enjoyed going to practice after a difficult day at school. She knew that one terrible day does not mean I definitely intended I wanted to   go   away the team. Sticking   to something and surely giving   it   your all suggests tenacity and   bravery.   If   there   comes   a time wherein you gave it your all and it is not what it used to be, then quitting may be reevaluated.

OVERLOOKING AWFUL MANNERS

Manners are there for a reason; humans playing others who're nicely-mannered.   How frustrating is it while the individual in front of you does not keep open the door? Or when   you sneeze   and no   one round you   says   "bless you!"? it's frustrating. It can feel like absolutely everyone is out for themselves. what   is worse   is while a child is ill-mannered   and a parent excuses their rudeness simply due to the fact they're a "toddler." while,   in fact,   being   a baby is the   appropriate age to learn manners! This
is while youngsters surely concentrate and attempt to be like father and   mother.
If mother   and   father forget
about their child's terrible manners, with   the   intention to continue for existence and   can make   it tough on   them   (and those round them).

IN   NO   WAY CORRECTING   THEM

I don't want to be the only to inform you this, but your baby isn't always usually right. they   may   be going to   wish their proper or say matters with   a   bit   of   luck to fit in   with   the verbal exchange, but that   doesn't imply that it   will paintings. In   case you're coaching your child numbers, and that they give you the incorrect solution, telling them they are correct is handiest hindering them. now not to mention making them feel assured in an area of take a look at in which they truly have to now not be confident in. Telling them they may be "right" all of the time can create an ego and fake encouragement. Be real along with your kids and let them recognize where they need to paintings difficult in

ANSWERING THEIR EACH CRY

when your little one falls at the ground, do you run over and assist them up? if you send your toddler to mattress for misbehaving, do you run into their room and surrender as soon as they start crying? nicely, tending in your infant's every cry is certainly a form of spoiling. there will come a time wherein you honestly cannot run to their room on every occasion they cry, and they're gonna have to discover ways to take delivery of that. they're going to should learn how to self-soothe themselves.

After they eventually become old, it's not like they are able to name Mom and cry on every occasion some thing goes wrong.

GETTING THEM A CAR SIMPLY BECAUSE THEY WANT IT

Buying a car is something that many Dad and Mom do for his or her young adults, and sure, it's very admirable. it's a luxurious that now   not many Dad   and Mom can afford,   so   if they   are able   to, shopping for their youngster a car may   be very 'cool parent' reputation. it's no   longer to mention that buying your child a car will lead   them to spoiled, however letting

them get anything automobile they want, now

not being grateful for the privilege, in trendy, could make them spoiled.   At   that   age,   a teen have   to be   thankful for any automobile they are able to drive. If they're kicking and crying   over   a vehicle that became sold particularly for them... it's one   spoiled,   ungrateful youngster.

OVERSPENDING ALL AROUND

Whilst i   used   to   be in center college,   all   I desired to do become healthy in.   I failed   to definitely have any style, however I   knew   what manufacturers had been trending. every Christmas, i would beg my Dad and Mom for all the   fashionable brands that the opposite youngsters were carrying, but alternatively, they would purchase me   a   knock-off version.   I in   no way understood why they might do this! I specially advised them what   I desired and   that   they got me   a cheaper model? Why? properly,   as   an person, i   can giggle at   my more youthful self because I certainly failed

to apprehend the cost of money.   My mother   and father attempted their quality to   make anyone satisfied with what they'd, and   that   i should have preferred that greater.

ALLOWING THEM TO REFUSE SOME MEALS

Unless you grew up eating leafy greens and vegetables from an early age, you're no longer going to select broccoli over pizza. Take me for example, there are foods I don't eat right ,because my body doesn't allow them, I hated some meals as a kid, and I was allowed not to eat them, and there was a handful of them. This affects me as an adult when I go for conferences, meetings and get together now. Kids are always going to want the junk ingredients. they're smooth, fun, and   tasty — what's no longer to   like! but, maximum of   those foods have no dietary cost. kids want to devour their culmination and veggies to benefit vitamins for   their growing our   bodies. It   is been documented by professionals time   and   time once more that children want those foods to develop strong. Simply bec ause a   child kicks and   screams   that   they want cake   over dinner doesn't imply they must receive what they're yearning after.   Dad and Mom have the closing say — not the other way around.

KEEP OVER PRAISING YOUR KIDS

There may be a distinction among helping and overpraising your child. Even though a determine wants to do their parenting responsibilities and cheer their youngster on, regardless of what, deep down they know while their infant doesn't need the praise. Telling them they may be the first-rate ones on the sphere (once you have final place) and that the judges don't have any idea what they're looking at is overpraising. Telling them they may be the great student within the college after coming domestic with an 'F' on their check is overpraising. It is a quality line, however a figure needs to be sensible. Cheering them on for doing so little does not sincerely upload up; it creates a fake feel of truth for them.

MAKING EMPTY THREATS

parents revel in being in strength. What they are saying goes. they could both make their baby's life extraordinarily clean or surprisingly hard; all the child desires to do is follow the regulations. Now, what a parent considers a threat is unique for anybody. No matter what it is even though, they want to follow through. In case you constantly inform them "in case you do not easy up your Legos, I'm going to throw you out" and by no means throw them out, this is an empty danger. They'll come a time where they do not take you seriously (because you've in no way thrown their Legos) and will keep to depart them out. simply how we take a look at the waters in special situations, kids are constantly trying out us. if you're going to make a subtle danger, follow thru with it.

INCONSISTENCY ISN'T   ALWAYS KEY

Kids want consistency in   their lifestyles; balance.   Having   an
inconsistent domestic lifestyles can   making such   things
as homework   or   after-faculty activities tough.
The children aren't sure who they   could trust or what   to
expect when   they cross domestic. as
the sleeping must be smooth blog says "you   spot,   it's   unfair
to anticipate your infant to know what to do while you've been
inconsistent.
He receives careworn whilst his obligations aren't clear, or in case
you don't constantly comply
with via with results." developing a recurring and sticking with it
is imperative in developing self-enough youngsters. this
will additionally help a infant learn   how   to accept   as   true
with greater and become secure in   their surroundings.

BRIBING   THEM

I   am now   not saying bribery doesn't work, because
it honestly does. in case you need your youngster to clean up their
room, telling them they will get $10 for doing so will cause them
to pop away   from   bed faster than   a cartoon man   or
woman. but, just like the dozing ought to be clean blog explains
"bribes are quick-term." She says "As bribes come to be the norm,
your child will begin   to assume better rewards earlier
than agreeing to do the assignment. Motivation wanes with each
time you need to convince her   to conform   to the   bribe." in
the lengthy-time period, this may additionally make your kid seek

for outside rewards in place of internal.

HANDING OUT CREDIT CARDS

Having an emergency credit card as a teen or younger grownup is extraordinarily famous. it's a way for mother and father to ease their minds when their youngster is out doing their very own issue. In case they need a journey somewhere or there may be an emergency scenario, they have Moms and Dad's bank account as a backup. If they may be the use of the emergency card for frivolous such things as clothes or espresso, it is while mum and Dad need to step in and take manipulate.

A exceptional manner to help your younger adult with their credit score card is coaching them approximately credit, too. maybe learning how it all works will make them think twice before swiping.

BELIEVING THEM PROPER AWAY OVER OTHER ADULTS

agree with is critical in any relationship. positive, your youngsters had been born trusting you however do you accept as true with them? There are a few Dad and Mom who blindly consider their toddler's words greater than all and sundry else's. They need to look at the bigger photograph, even though.

If a instructor explains they noticed this particular student searching off any other student's take a look at or plagiarizing a paper, a parent wishes to take that information with a grain of salt and handle the state of affairs wisely at home. completely ignoring what the teacher had informed them and in no way discussing it with their infant is a positive fire manner to have your child experience like they are able to do and say something.

ALWAYS PROTECT THEM FROM TOUGH TIMES

No one desires to be burdened or go through hard times. all of us need to stay in a bubble where nothing awful occurs to us. it truly is not real lifestyles, although. Existence is full of ups and downs, and it's a discern responsibility to train their child how to address it.

it is understandable when a parent most effective needs their baby to be round positive, uplifting things, however this is not continually the case. They'll sense like they are protecting their youngster from damage, but what they're really doing is secluding them from reality. knowing each the good and bad matters going on inside the world can assist a child study their purpose in life.

IDENTIFYING THEIR FUTURE FOR THEM

I recognize some families who already knew what their child changed into going to be after they "grew up" entirely as it become their dream — no longer their child's dream. similarly, if a child sees how a lot their mother and father need them to be a doctor, they're going to strive their hardest to be a doctor. but it is now not what they wanted — it's what their mother and father wanted. This, in turn, can create a resentful toddler who's most effective going approximately their destiny for the sake of their parent's happiness. it is top notch having all this guide when deciding on a field of look at, but as a figure, selecting their destiny for them doesn't permit much time for independence and mirrored image.

MAKING SURE THEY' ARE THE BEST

As youngsters, we are typically shoved into sports to see which suits; what we're maximum attracted to. however whilst dear old father and mother make their aggressive nature their whole existence, it truly is whilst it could grow to be a trouble.
A infant is not horseback riding because they like it, they're doing it due to the fact they feel like they want to "outdo" other people they realize. even if Dad and Mom are leaving $a hundred payments beneath the pillow from the tooth Fairy! this can make a kid feel like they may be better than all people else when they listen different children their age get a dollar from the tooth Fairy.

three things it's time to prevent Doing in

your youngsters proper Now

maximum Dad and Mom try to be the nice mother and

father they can be. however some of their actions can be doing extra damage than exact. now could be the time to make some changes and kick some terrible conduct to the scale back. right here are 33 belongings you want to prevent doing these days.

FEELING LIKE YOU'RE FAILING

Although it's not unusual for parents to be tough on themselves, that kind of wondering is counterproductive. in place of beating your self up, take a look at the little missteps as an possibility to develop and study.

Understand that some days may be higher than others—that it's absolutely regular to make bad parenting choices or to your children to misbehave.

Permit your kids to peer you're making errors and research from them. Demonstrating a increase attitude to your own lifestyles is a brilliant manner to teach them to be resilient and persevere of their personal life.

DOING THE ENTIRETY FOR THEM

With a purpose to make your kids' lives less difficult, you'll be doing them a disservice. The excellent way to elevate impartial children is to allow them to practice being independent.

So what if milk receives spilled onto the counter rather than making it into the glass because you failed to step in to help? kids can study lots by using trying things on their own. Plus, allowing them to try to master new capabilities suggests them which you consider in them, and that helps construct self assurance.

NEGLECTING YOUR MARRIAGE

It is clean to end up so centered on raising your youngsters, looking after them, and ensuring they may be satisfied that you forget about one in every of your maximum critical relationships—your marriage. Nurture your partnership by means of making plans date nights together, connecting with every other every day, and taking the time to talk before delivering at night time.

It's also critical to your kids to see you doing things together. So regularly make time for your accomplice despite the fact that it is just sitting at

the couch and talking. ensure your youngsters understand that this is your unique time together and that they have to chorus from interrupting   if in   any   respect feasible.

Your kids want to recognize that   your   marriage   is a   priority.

COMBATING OVER LITTLE MATTERS

You cannot win every warfare and   also   you should   not try to. pick your parenting battles wisely. The little things clearly do not count   number. in   case   your preschooler wants to put on a plaid blouse with polka dot pants, let them rock that mismatched outfit. some matters just are not well worth fighting over.

Plus, it is laborious to have a war over each little selection. look

for possibilities to   mention sure while you   can.

This manner, while it   comes   time to   mention no,

your kids are greater receptive in   your choice.

NEGLECTING   TO
ASSIGN OBLIGATIONS

Many children have   a
carefree lifestyles with 0 obligations. that's a great luxury to
bestow to   your baby. but it also approach that   all of
the responsibilities likely fall   on   you.   It additionally may lead
your child to become irresponsible, in particular as they get older.

Assigning age-suitable chores teaches

your children the significance of contributing to the household.

Provide your self a destroy by delegating a number of your household responsibilities to

your youngsters. teaching youngsters vital lifestyles skills and

giving them chores is part of supporting them emerge

as a accountable person sooner or later.

NOT GIVING THEM BREATHING SPACE

We need our youngsters to revel in lifestyles, discover ways to do new things,

and experience everything they need. however that also can lead to over-scheduling them. withstand the urge to cram sports activities, dance, piano instructions, scouts, and other sports into their lives at one time. no longer most effective will you run yourself ragged, over-scheduling

your kids doesn't supply them any free time to just be children.

Research indicates that unstructured play can

have a fine impact on a child's improvement and well-

being. whilst children are given the opportunity to play freely,

there is lots of gaining knowledge of taking region.

They develop games, make policies, negotiate with others,

and launch pressure.

PUTTING YOUR DESIRES ON HOLD

Dad and Mom often unwittingly placed themselves in a function of doing the whole lot for every person else. however this can be emotionally and bodily draining and lead to frustration, irritability, and burnout. it is critical to make time for activities you revel in and to practice self-care. it's useful for you, but also in your family.

it's right on your children to peer you embracing your hobbies, taking care of your self, and scheduling time together with your pals. you'll be a more fit, satisfied figure and keep away from burnout if you prioritize your very own desires simply as a great deal as you do your circle of relatives.

BINGE ON BLUE LIGHT DEVICES

There may be no denying that technology has grow to be an indispensable part of our lives. whether it is at work, for faculty, or truly maintaining up with circle of relatives and friends, everyone is based on era to get matters accomplished. but it's critical to have some time apart from generation to truly be with your family individuals. Think about the ultimate time you unplugged your gadgets to spend one-on-one time with your child. To assist make it easier to unplug, take into account growing gadget-loose times and zones in your home. it may take a concerted attempt, but in the long run it'll be beneficial for every body if you all have some generation-unfastened time together.

TRYING TO BE TOGETHER 24/7

Determine guilt is a real element and not uncommon. a few mother and father even guilt themselves into seeking to spend each waking Moment with their youngsters. but not only is that this now not humanly feasible, it is also no longer healthful. As an alternative, try to revel in excellent time together with your circle of relatives, however also recognize the significance of letting your children play alone or with their siblings. not only will time aside permit your youngsters to develop autonomy and independence, however it also will lift a burden from you as nicely. anybody wishes a few alone time. You can't be all things in your toddler. it's vital that they start to broaden friendships and relationships with others too.

SPOILING THOSE TEENAGERS

Most parents would like for their kids to be happy one hundred% of the time; however this expectation is unrealistic. but, this doesn't stop mother and father from attempting.

And when this happens, mother and father grow to be inadvertently spoiling their youngsters. Material things are excellent, however they don't bring lasting happiness. Educate your youngsters to discover pleasure in much less fabric methods and you will be nicely on your manner to elevating an amazing citizen.

As opposed to giving in on your infant's whims or shopping

for them the whole

lot they need, recognition on coaching them how

to locate contentment in serving others, operating difficult,

and going after their dreams.

FORGETTING   TO TRAIN GRATITUDE

Overall,   if you   are   like maximum Dad   and Mom, you're probably quite skilled at teaching your children to say "please"   and write thank   you notes, however do your children recognize what   it simply approach to be grateful? Make sure the phrases they're speaking are not empty.

Make an effort to enhance grateful youngsters who appreciate everything and everybody round them is considered one of your maximum important jobs   as   a parent. Being grateful allows youngsters to   step out   of   doors in their personal self-interests and apprehend that they   may   be no longer entitled   to   all the   great   things in   their existence. coaching your toddler gratitude starts with   getting   them to see that due to the fact not anything in existence is promised, they ought to be grateful for all that is right of their world.

LOOKING   TO BE   LIKE OTHER DAD AND   MOM

TikTok, Facebook, the bragging mother next door, and the pressure we put on ourselves have all became parenthood into a blood game. Too often, parents compare themselves to others—and accept as true with that they are arising short. Whether you are trying to fulfill others' expectancy or lack self assurance, imitating others may be harmful to you and even make a contribution to figure shaming and judgmental attitudes. as a substitute, cognizance on coming across who you are as a discern and stay authentic to those goals. at the same time as it's exceptional to research from other mother and father, it's also critical to be real for your values and dreams.

FORCING FRIENDSHIPS ON THEM

The flip side of now not liking your children's buddies takes place whilst you end up forcing any other baby in your very own kid. You agenda play dates, enroll them within the identical activities, and pester your child to text them due to the fact you are simply so giddy approximately this friendship. but, in case your baby is less captivated with the friendship than you are, you want to lighten up.

Whilst it is exceptional to assist them set up friendships, forcing your baby into a courting with someone that they don't connect with will in the long run result in failure.

Let your infant take the lead on who they befriend and spend time with. as long as the person they pick out isn't a bully or conducting peer pressure, it's possibly a appropriate friendship.

BLOWING UP AT THEM

One among your children shoved a paperclip into the light transfer. some other climbed the pantry and helped themself to a bag of marshmallows. Your final straw become when your toddler controlled to present the dog a new hairdo with baby lotion.

Parenting may be irritating, no question. but blowing up at your children is not the solution. forestall yelling and discover a higher manner to speak with them so they may genuinely concentrate to what you have to say.

NEGLECTING THE LITTLE MOMENTS

Do your first-class to sluggish down and recognize the little matters in your baby's existence. earlier than you understand it, they'll be a hectic teen and then heading off to college. Consciously take a breath and enjoy looking your infant colour or all your youngsters running together to build the most important citadel.

Remind yourself, too, that you don't need massive vacations or luxurious toys to create circle of relatives memories. some of your quality   reminiscences   can   also come   from mundane events like cooking   dinner together,   raking   leaves in the fall, or gambling playing cards on a rainy summer season night time.

FORCING   THEM   TO EAT

I know this sounds like a contradiction as I said earlier not to let them choose what they can eat. There is a thin line between letting them eat what they want to eat, and not forcing them to eat. If you're   like maximum mother   and   father, you need your kids to eat healthful foods and
you possibly visit first-
rate attempt to provide nutritious alternatives for them. however if your children gag on   every   occasion they chunk into a green bean, there   is an   awesome danger that irrespective of how tough you attempt, you   are now   not going to exchange their meals options.

Instead   of forcing   them   to devour ingredients they do not like, divulge them   to   many   flavors and textures without requiring   them   to consume some thing. offer nutritious alternatives that   you realize they   do like along much   less favored or familiar ones. if   they insist they don't like a sure meals, forcing them to eat it's far placing you up   for   a warfare nobody goes to   win.

You   are one person.   You can   not stitch the   costumes   for the magnificence play, train three days a   week for every one among your kid's sports   activities teams,   and   bake three hundred cupcakes for the faculty bake sale in two days.

Help out in your phrases and do not succumb to guilt. Volunteer at your infant's school as soon as a month rather of every week. Be the crew figure as   soon   as a year alternatively of   each season for all   your children.   You truly can't say yes to the   whole thing and it   is important which   you vicinity some limits   on how regularly you   get involved.

COMPARING YOUR CHILDREN TO OTHERS

Parents naturally have   a   tendency to compare their youngsters to others. but it   is unfair. it   is   able   to cause   them to feel guilty for now not having the identical successes as others. And it   is   able   to harm their   relationships   with   the human beings you are evaluating them to.

Comparisons among siblings, for instance, can gasoline sibling competition or   even cause sibling   bullying. no   person wants to be in comparison to each person else, in particular kids who're still seeking to parent out who they are.

Rather, try to discover the beauty and uniqueness in each of your youngsters without comparing them to everybody else. whilst you let your kids recognize what makes them unique, you are helping to construct their self-self belief.

"Do I have to take a shower tonight?" my son asked with a balk on his face. there has been no P.E. that day and he hadn't gotten sweaty, so I said, "Nah. but please get in the bathtub and wash your ft. They're grimy and grimy feet result in grimy carpets." His reaction became, "Meh, we'll just get new carpets." His brother concurred. Excuse me? just buy new carpets? How did I increase such spoiled kids?

To conclude, there are no manuals to being a mother, or a father, but you have experienced childhood, and know what worked for you, and what did not. Apply these things with wisdom, knowing that every child is unique, and in all you do, always make sure they know you love, and whatever you are doing are for their own benefit, even if they are not seeing it now.

www.ingramcontent.com/pod-product-compliance
Lightning Source LLC
Chambersburg PA
CBHW051942150726

47999CB00006B/2338